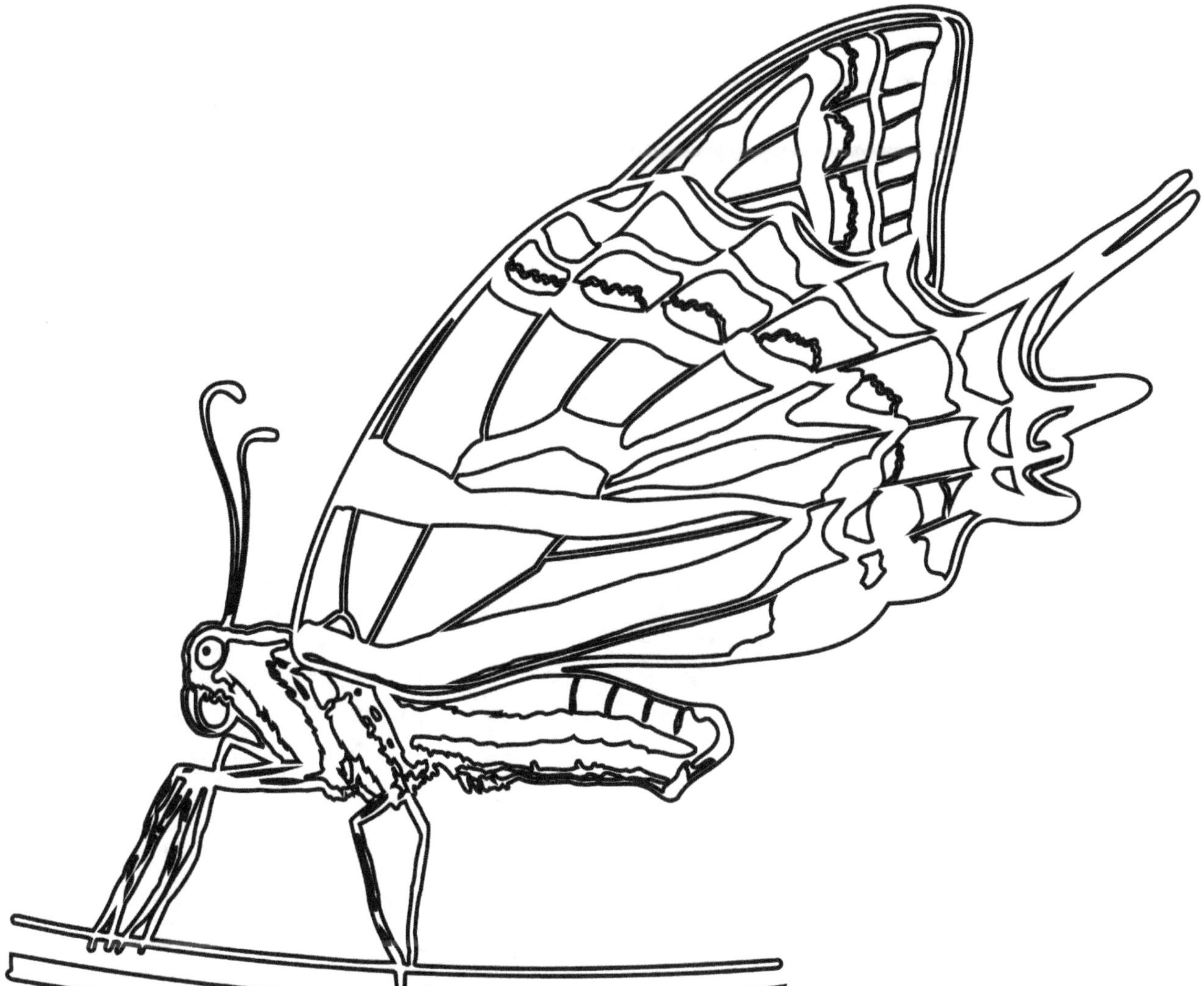

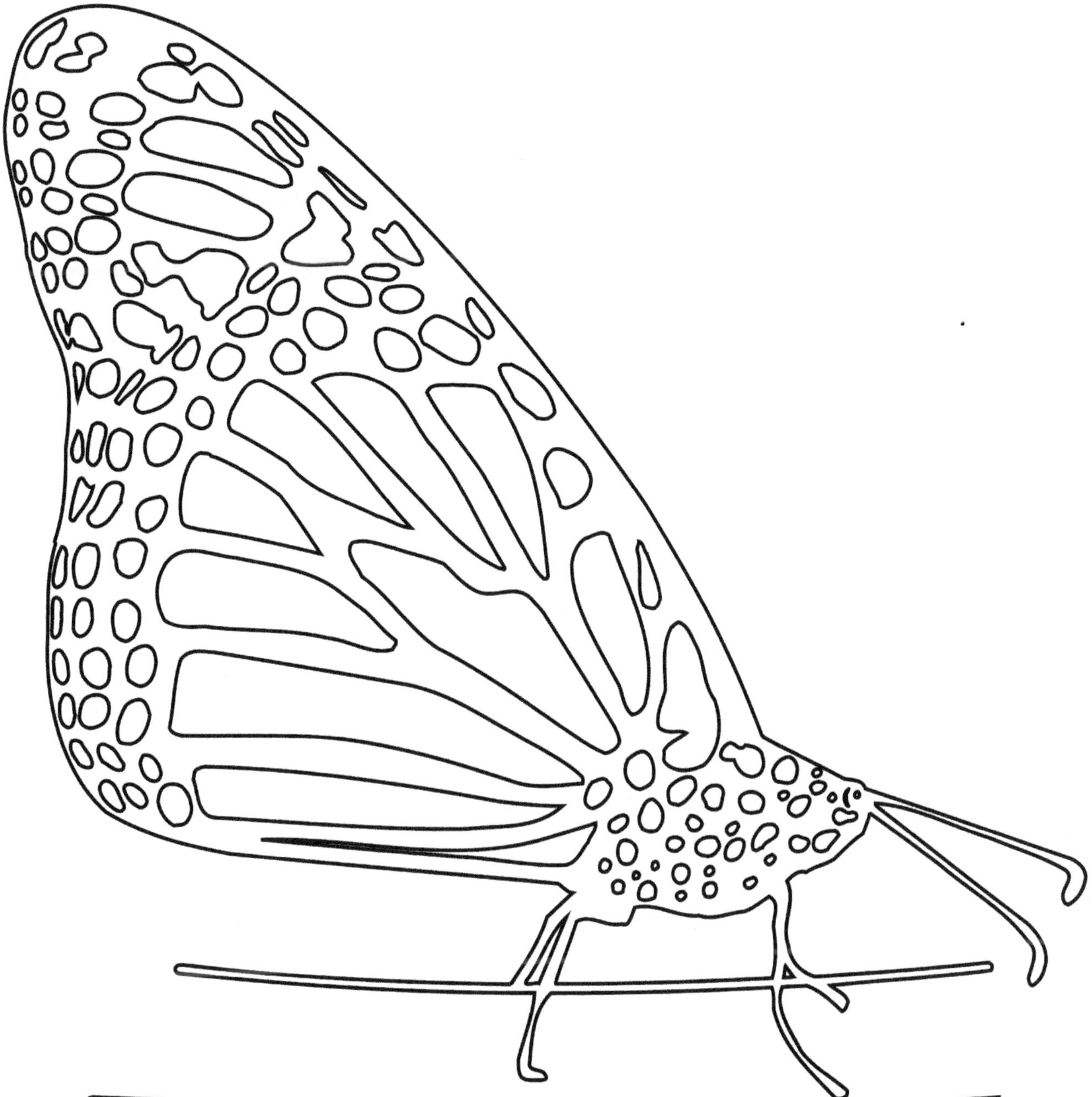

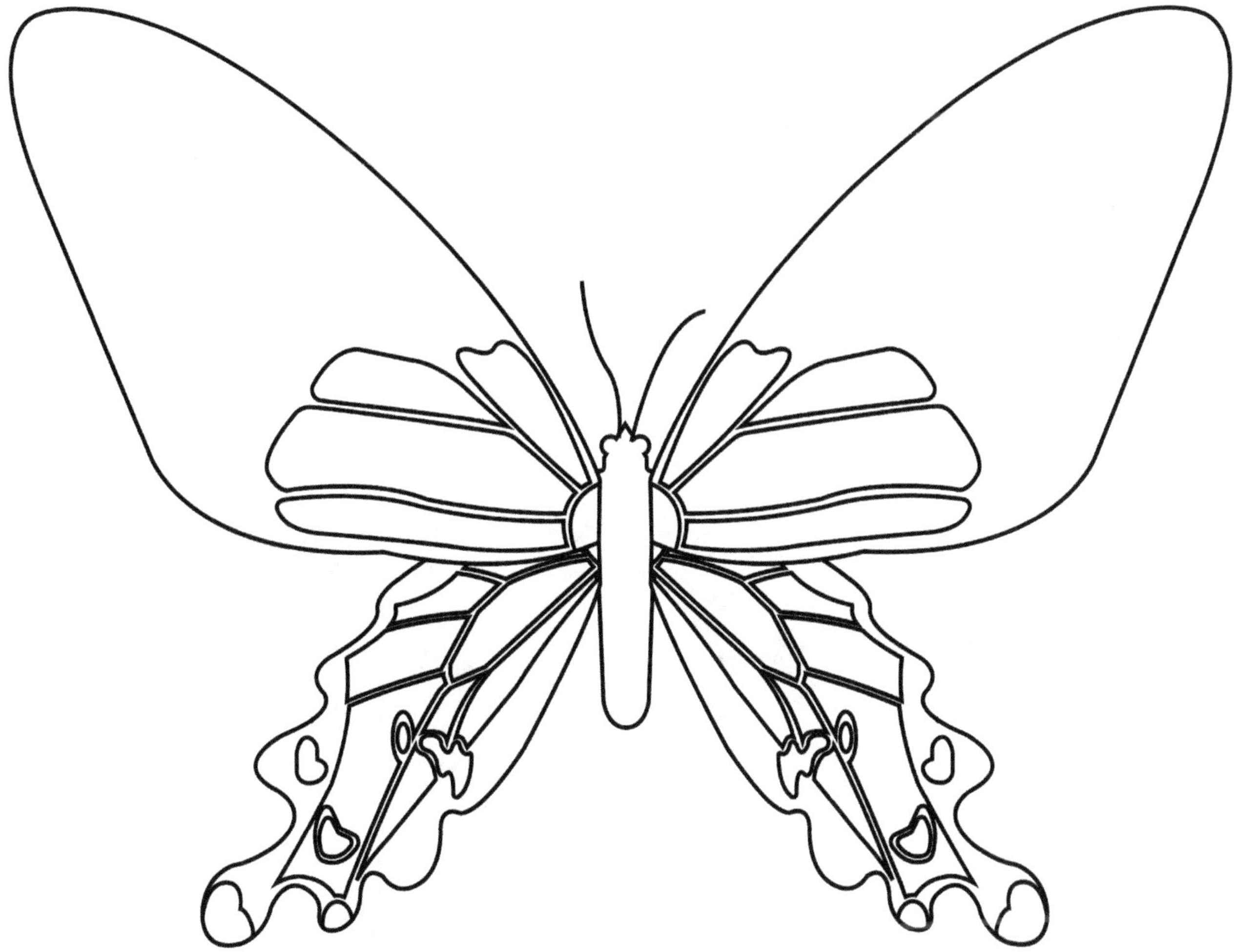

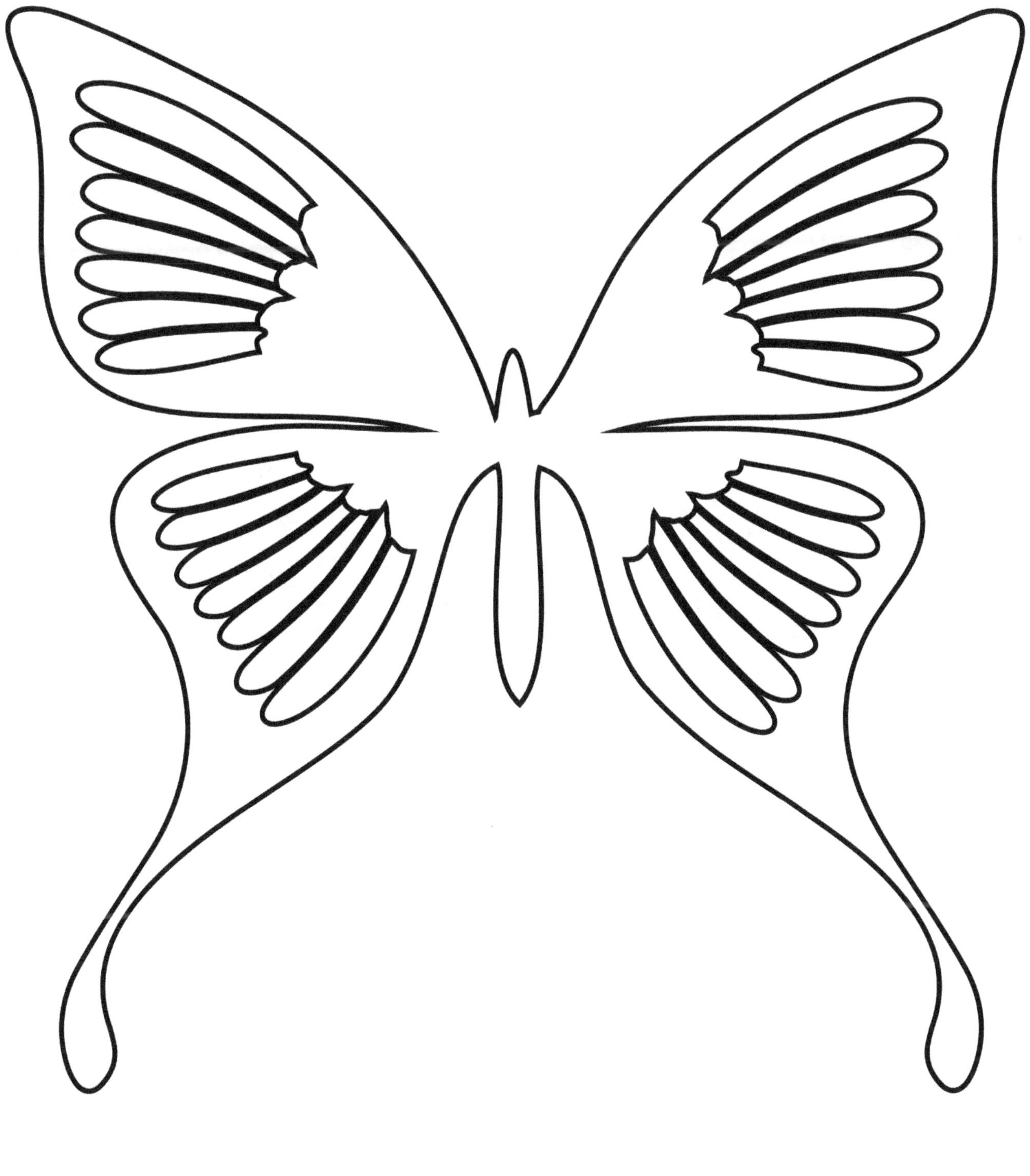

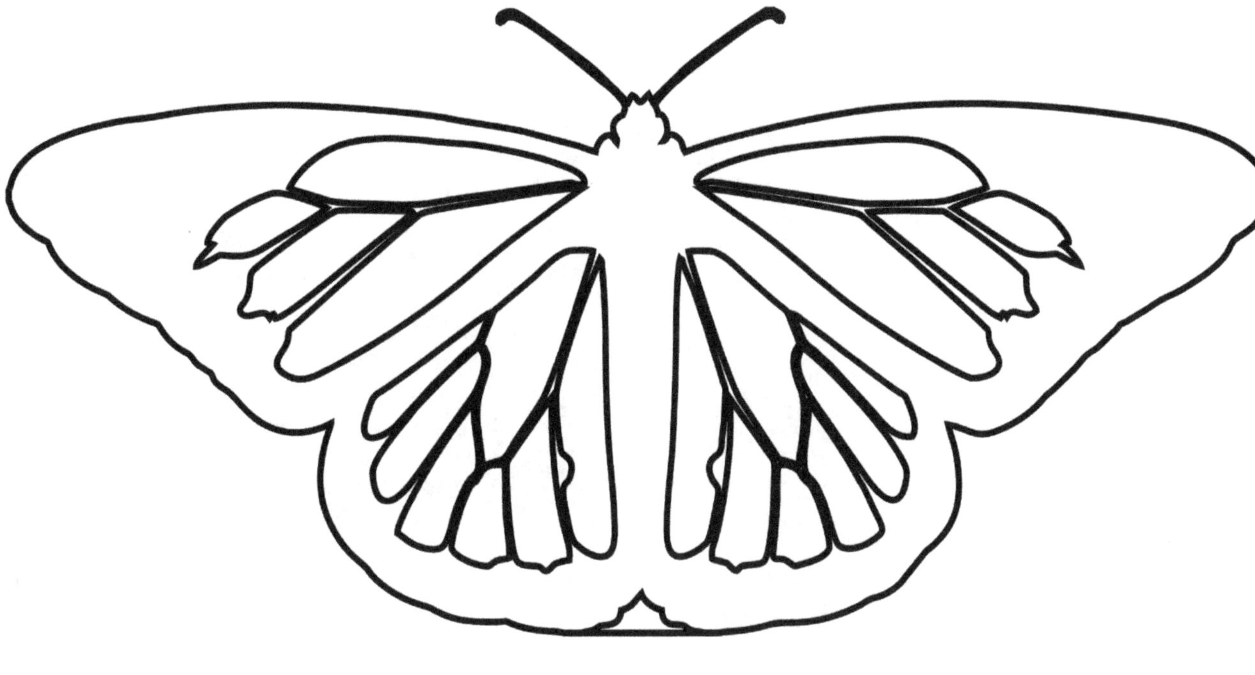

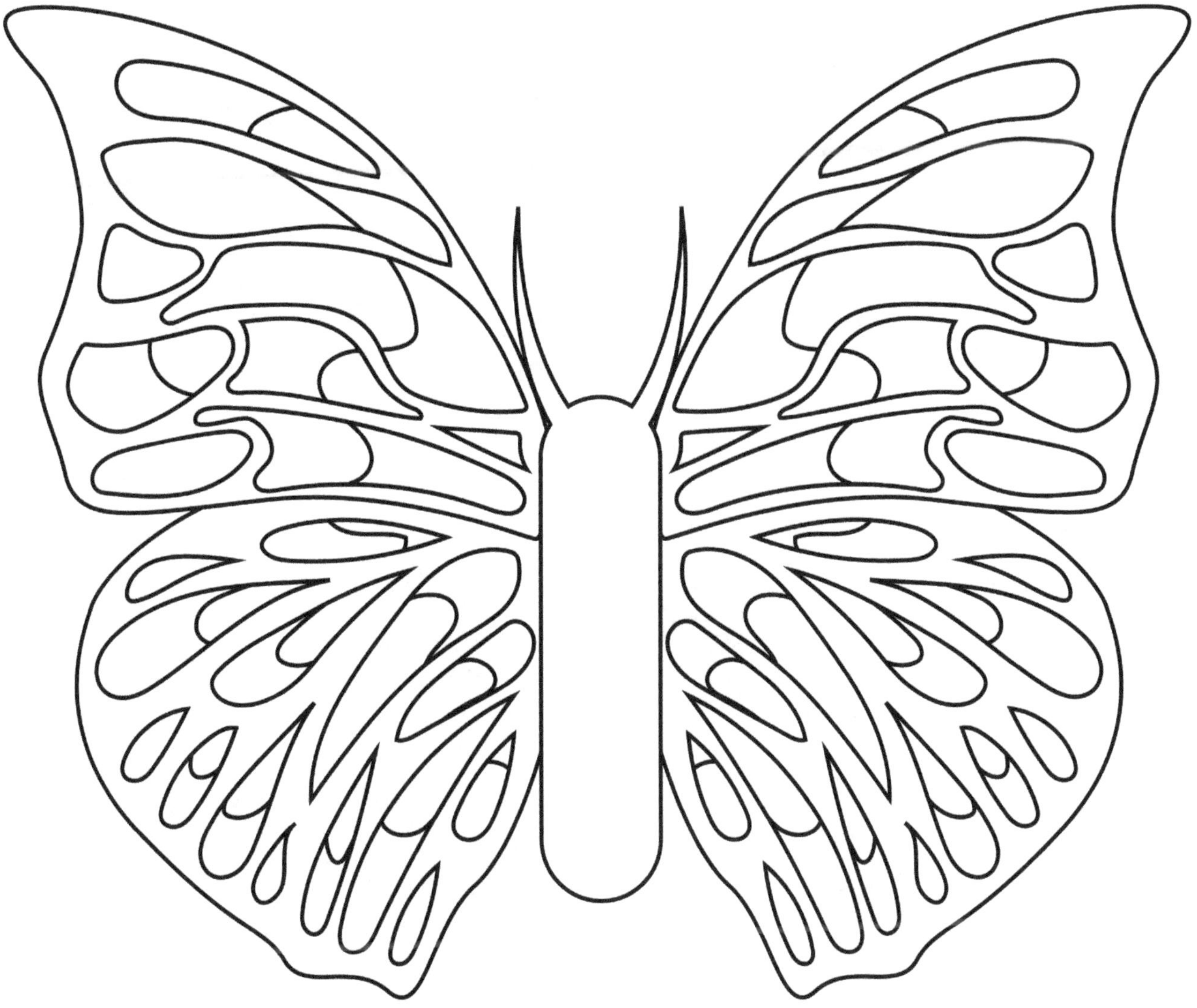

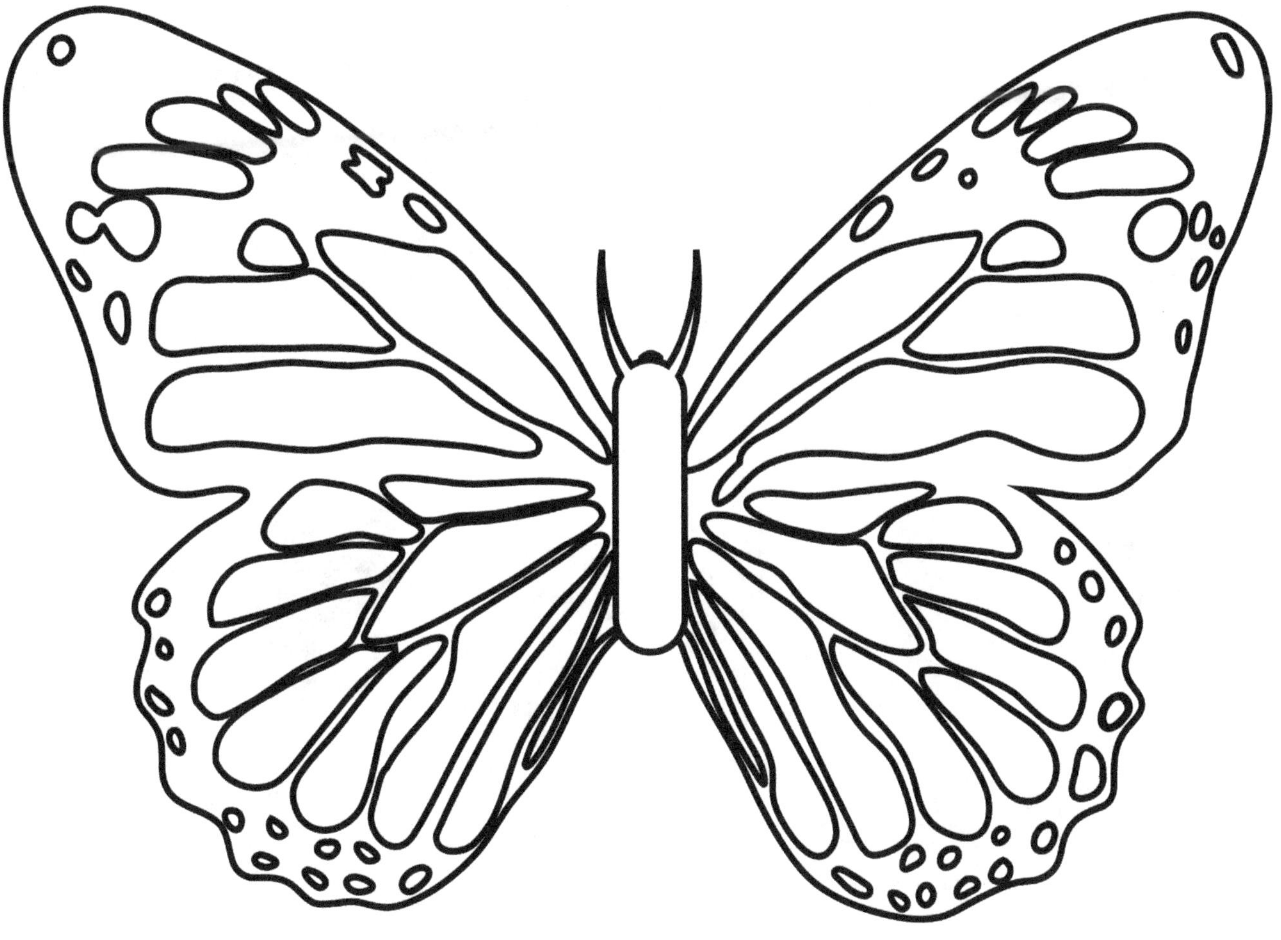

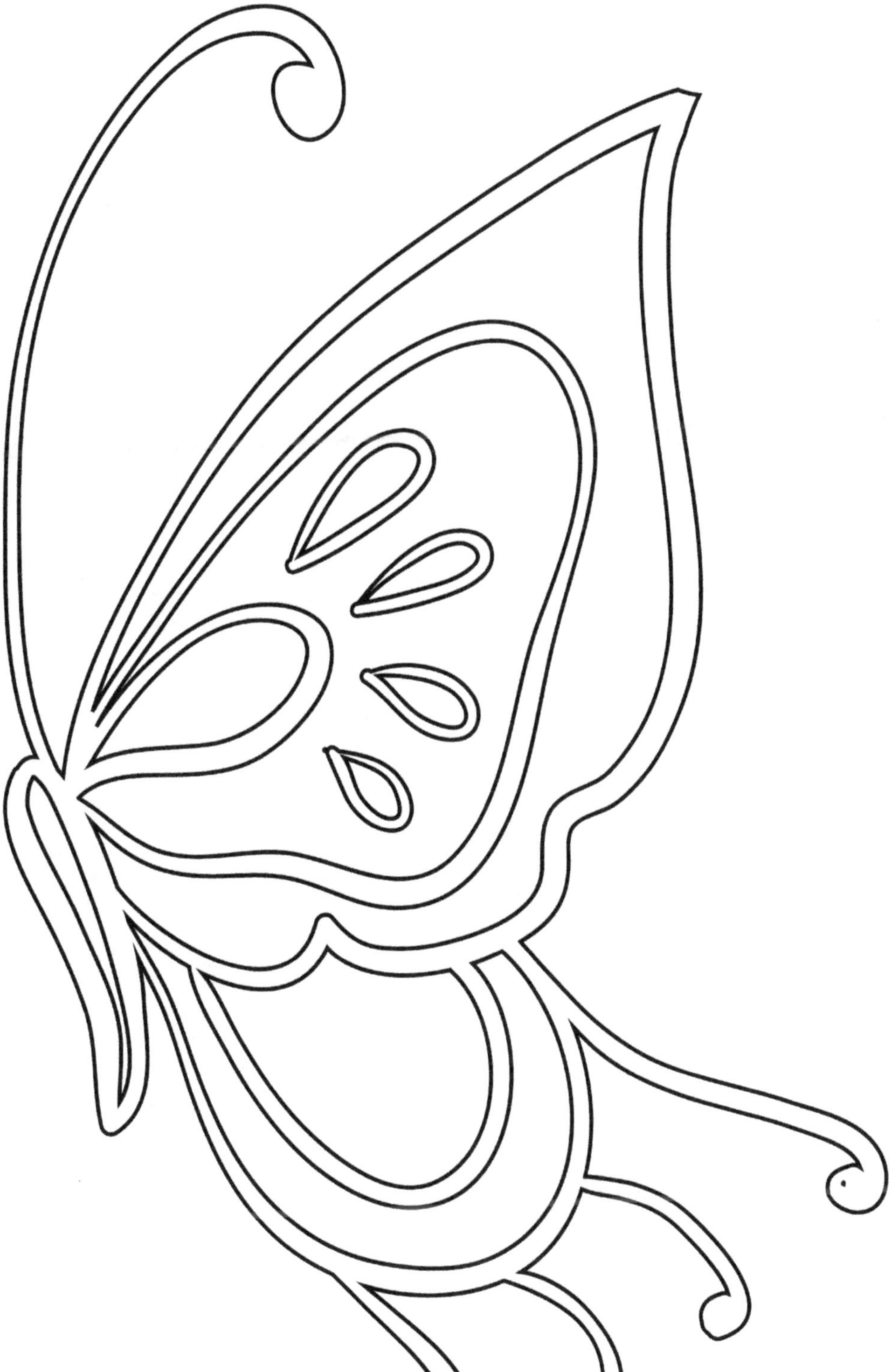

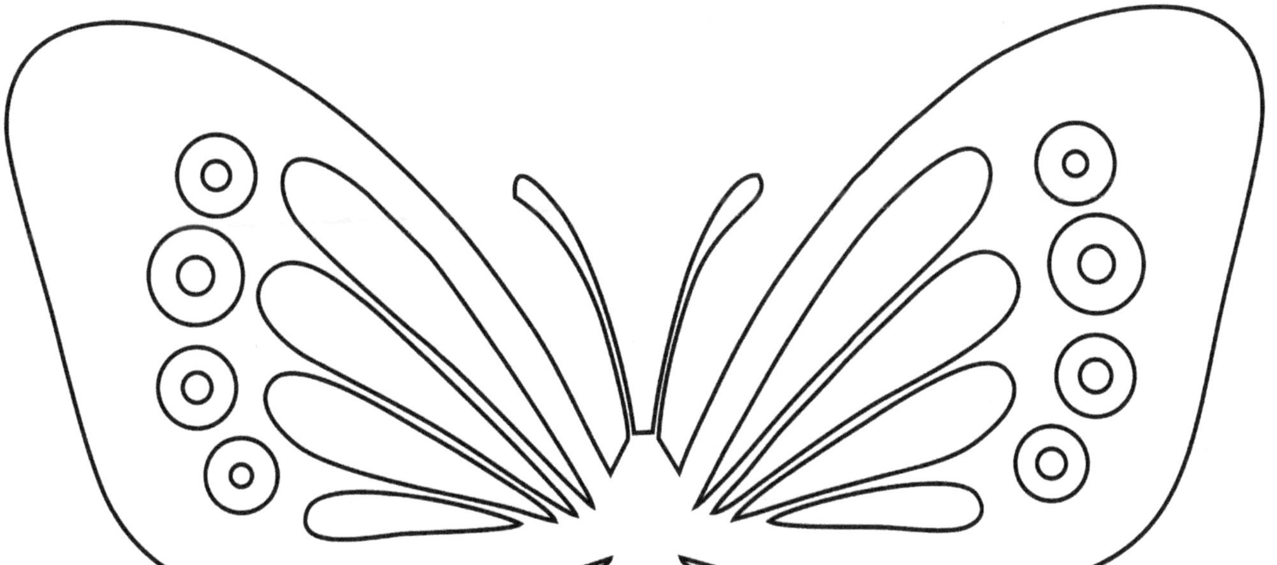

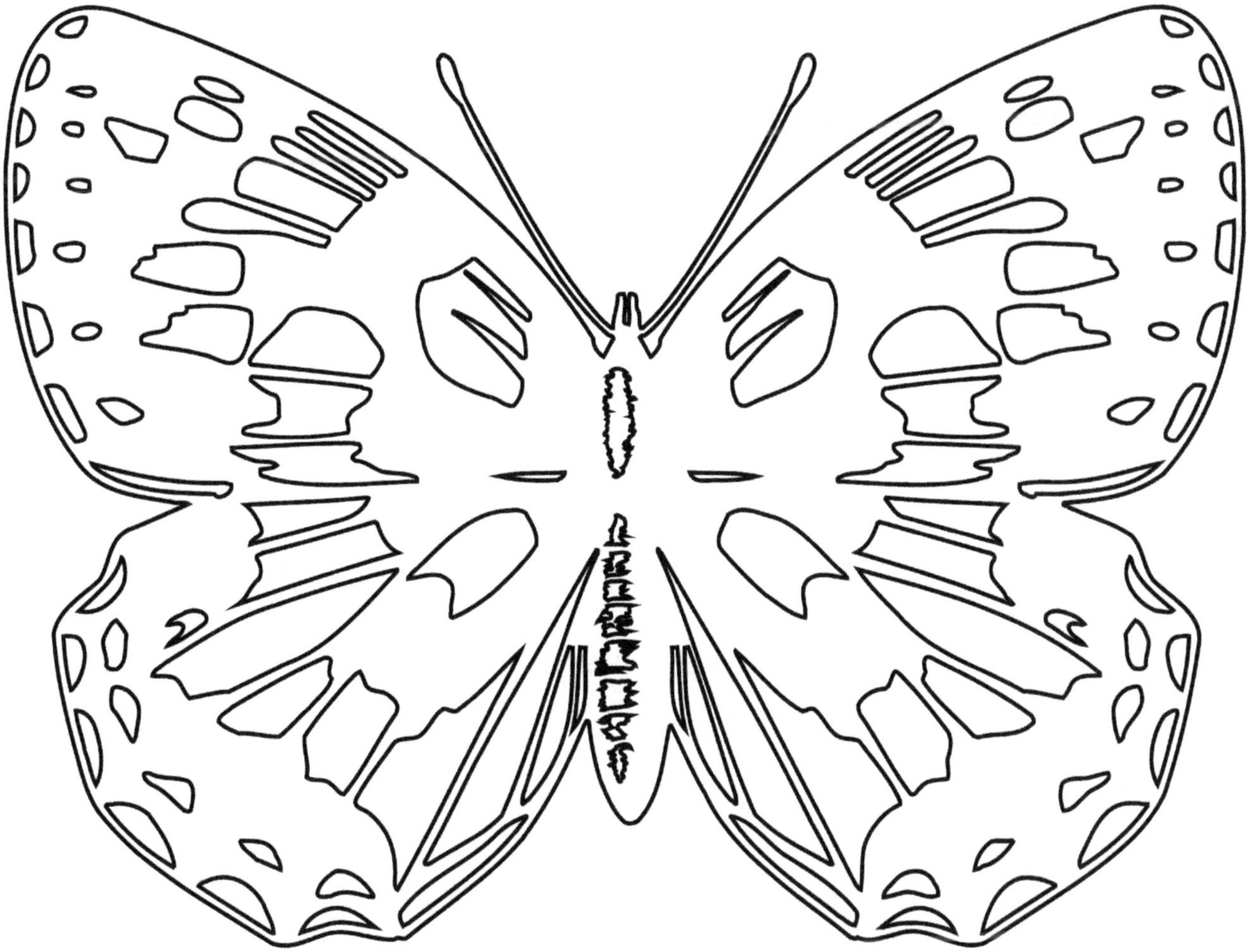

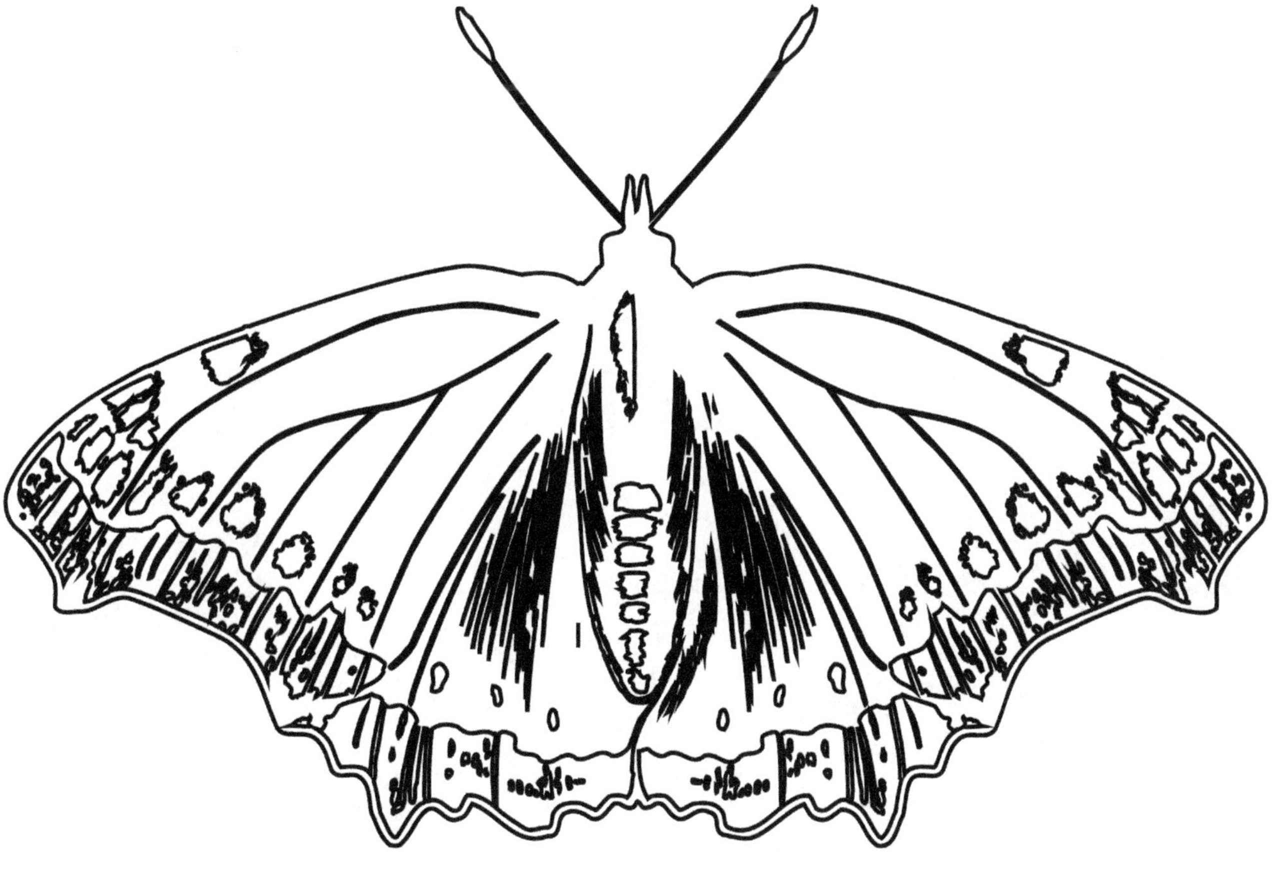

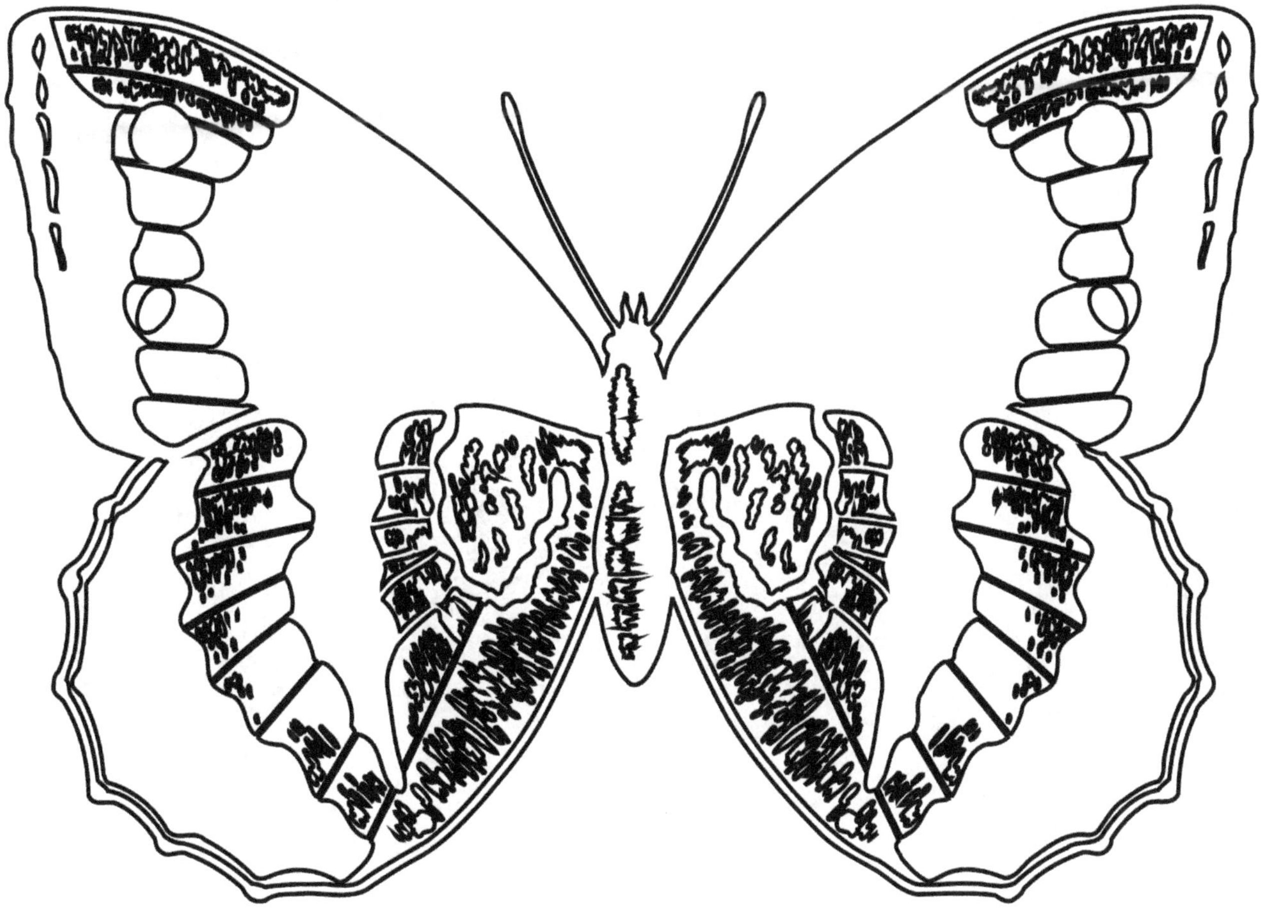

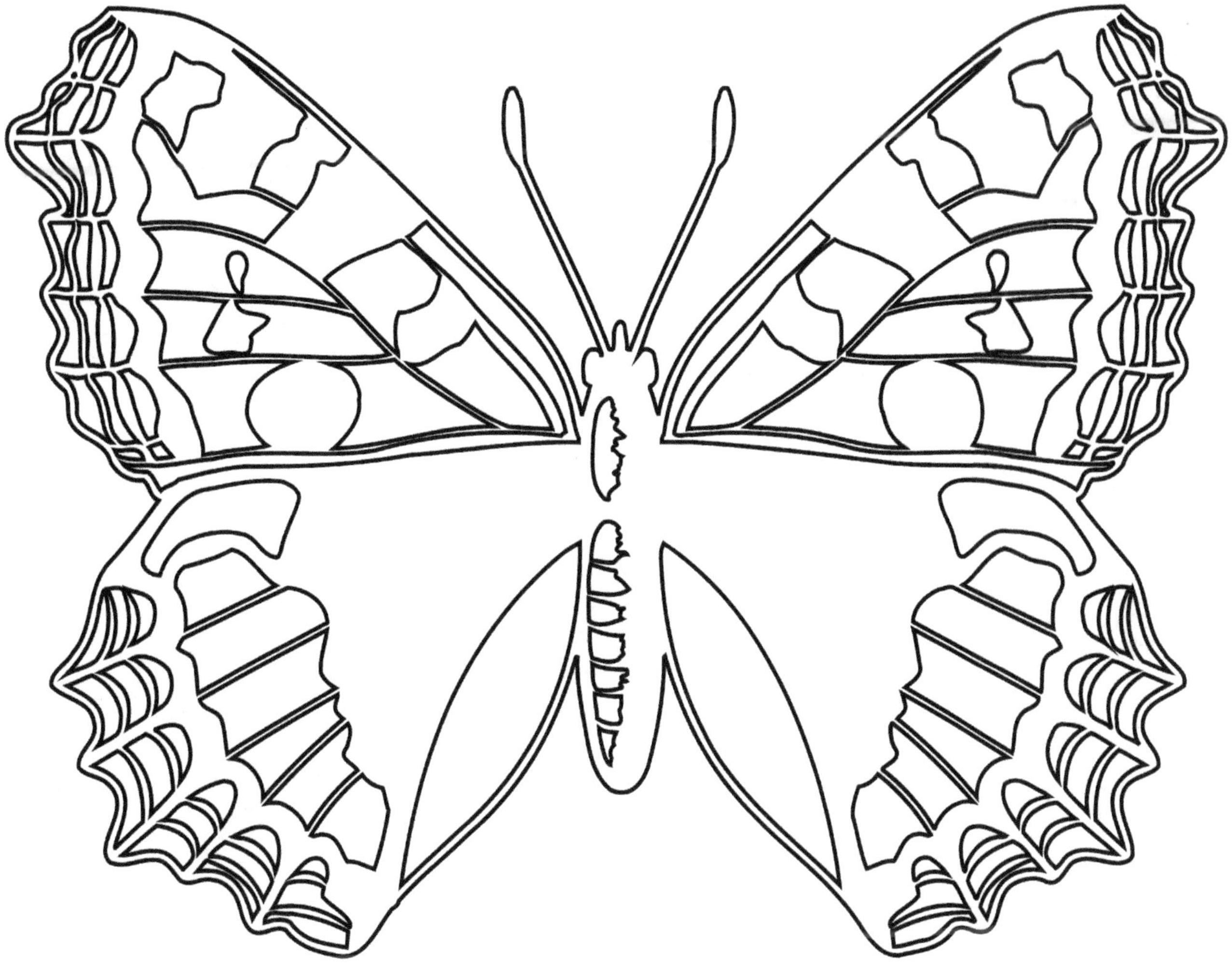

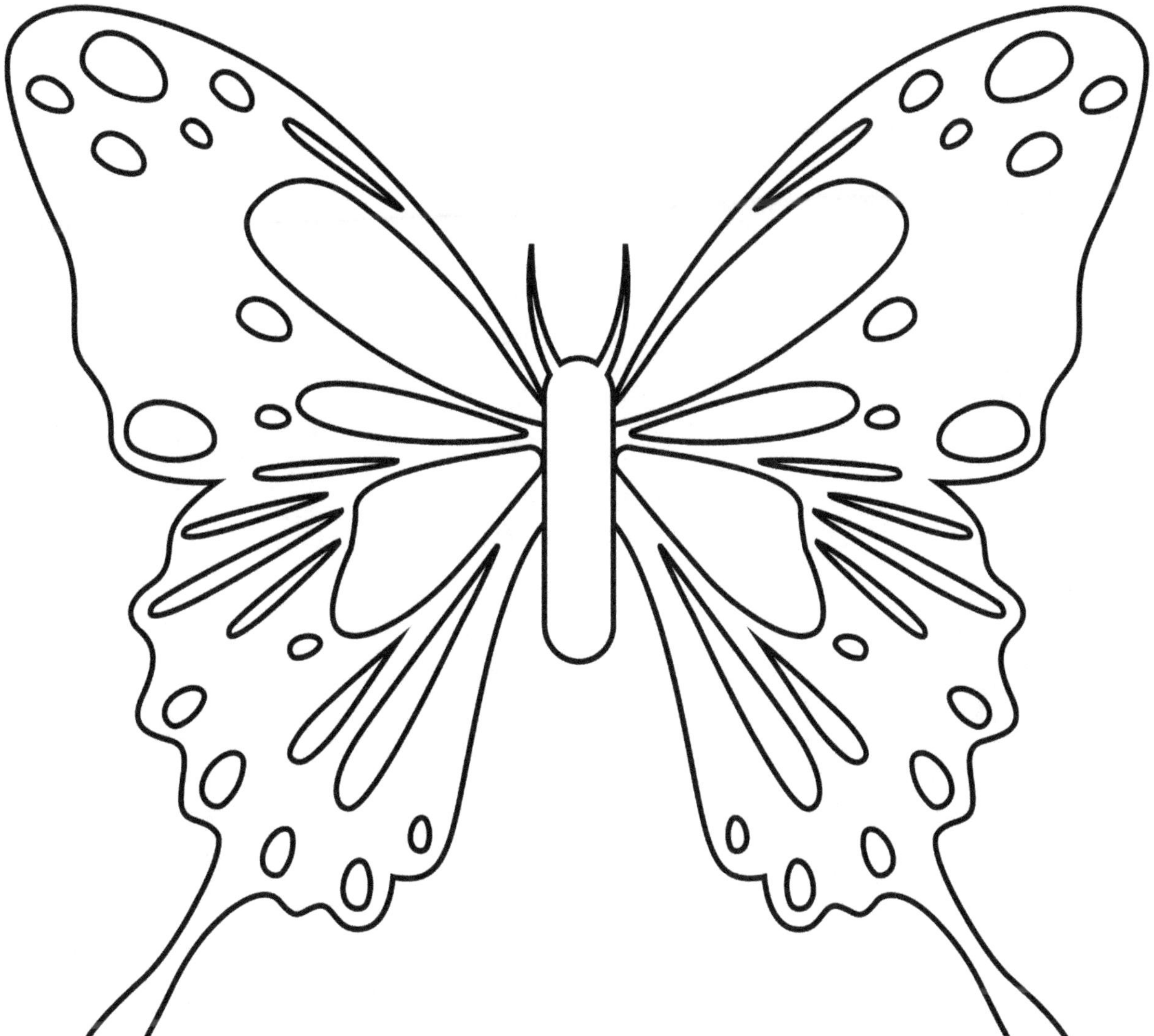

CPSIA information can be obtained
at www.ICGtesting.com
Printed in the USA
BVHW090033260221
601128BV00010B/1033

9 781801 826259